This book belongs to

_____

...a boy who wants to make really good choices!

A BOY'S GUIDE TO MAKING REALLY GOOD CHOICES

JIM GEORGE

HARVEST HOUSE PUBLISHERS
EUGENE, OREGON

Cover by Dugan Design Group, Bloomington, Minnesota

HARVEST KIDS is a registered trademark of The Hawkins Children's LLC. Harvest House Publishers, Inc., is the exclusive licensee of the federally registered trademark HARVEST KIDS.

A BOY'S GUIDE TO MAKING REALLY GOOD CHOICES
Copyright © 2013 by Jim George
Published by Harvest House Publishers
Eugene, Oregon 97408
www.harvesthousepublishers.com

Library of Congress Cataloging-in-Publication Data
George, Jim
A boy's guide to making really good choices / Jim George.
    p. cm.
ISBN 978-0-7369-5518-8 (pbk.)
ISBN 978-0-7369-5519-5 (eBook)
        1. Boys—Conduct of life. 2. Boys—Religious life. 3. Choice (Psychology)—Religious aspects—Christianity. 4. Decision making—Religious aspects—Christianity. I. Title.
BJ1461.G46 2013
248.8'32—dc23
                                                                        2013012862

Printed in the United States of America
                17 18 19 20 21 / VP-JH / 12 11 10 9 8

*It is with great pride and thanksgiving
to our Lord that this book is lovingly
dedicated to my four grandsons, my "boys":*

*Jacob Seitz
Matthew Zaengle
Isaac Seitz
Ryan Zaengle*

*It is such a joy to see the four of you
loving God and desiring to make choices
based on His Word. I love you and
pray diligently for each of you.*

Contents

You Have a Choice

1

oy, does it ever feel great to get out of school. What a day! Justin thought to himself as he proudly unlocked the chain that protected his Huffy ZRX terrain bike. (You know the one—the black bike with the words "ZRX Extreme Racer Series" boldly stenciled on the chain guard. Yeah, that one!)

As Justin continued right on with his thinking while he backed away from the bike rack at McKinley Middle School, he couldn't help but think, *Most days are okay, but today seemed like a train wreck right from the get-go.* For Justin, the downward spiral started in the morning when he told his mom that he had forgotten to set his alarm clock the previous night.

Well, it was sort of the truth. Justin had *meant* to set his clock, but he remembered to do so only after he had gotten in bed. And because the clock was all the way across his room—all of seven feet away!—he chose to let his mom wake him as she usually did whenever he "forgot" to set his alarm. Normally this was not a big deal, except today his dad was going on an important business trip and his mother was trying to help him get away on time to catch his plane. *Soooo,*

Justin told himself, *it was really my mom's fault that I was late for school!*

Justin tried hard to put the scene of his mother's disappointment behind him. At the same time, he was trying to forget the look on Mrs. Adams's face when he told her he had forgotten his English assignment and left it at home and promised to bring it tomorrow. (Actually, this was not a lie. He had "forgotten" his paper—forgotten to write it!) His mom had reminded him about it last night, as she had done for the last several days.

So what happened? Justin had gotten so involved in a video game that he completely forgot about doing his English assignment.

So now Justin was pedaling his way home on the coolest bike ever made. His mission? To dash off something to turn in tomorrow. Sure, he would get a lower grade, but something would be better than nothing, right? Even if it came with just a little lie.

But wait—hadn't Ryan mentioned something about meeting him and some of his other buddies at their secret clubhouse for a look at a new electronic game? Never mind Justin's parents had told him not to hang out with Ryan. They had explained that Ryan was older and was, according to their opinion, beginning to wrongly influence Justin's behavior.

I don't get it. What's so wrong with Ryan? Justin wondered as he pedaled along. Ryan's a neat guy. His parents buy him all those cool video games, and Justin looked up to him because he was older and knew "stuff"—*lots* of stuff!

So off Justin rode to join the gang at their secret club-house, patting himself on the back and thinking everything would be just fine. He promised himself he wouldn't stay long. Besides, who would know he had been there?

Fun in God's Word!

As we begin putting together our guide for making really good choices, you already know that life is full of choices. In fact, you have made a choice to start reading this book! Well, maybe you didn't have a choice. Maybe your mom or dad or Sunday school teacher or youth leader chose this book for you and the guys to read. So it's not really your choice. I'm sure you enjoy it more when you can make a choice about what you do. My hope is that as you continue reading, you'll enjoy this book more and more.

It's time now to see what God's Word, the Bible, says about choices. In this part of each chapter, we will look at Bible verses and answer some questions about the topics covered in the chapter. Our goal is to let God teach us about how to make really good choices. So go find a pen and be ready to write down some answers as you look up some verses in the Bible. As we go through the questions below, we are going to spell out the word C-H-O-I-C-E-S.

Yes, life is full of choices. Right now there are a lot of people in your life who are making choices for you, and that's a good thing. The people who care about you are looking out for you—like your parents, your schoolteachers, your Sunday school teacher, and many others. Now, it's true that you have no choice about where you live, where you go to school, what you study, when you must go to bed, and on it goes. But whether you make your own choices or others make them for you, there are important things involved in making choices.

Choices deal with your heart. There are lots of choices that you and boys like Justin can and will make for yourself. They are choices that deal with your heart, which then affect your attitudes and ultimately your actions. What do these verses say about your heart attitude?

> *Above all else, guard your heart, for everything you do flows from it* (Proverbs 4:23).

God's command: _____

Why? _____

_____

> *A good man brings good things out of the good stored up in his heart, and an evil man brings evil things out of the evil stored up in his heart* (Luke 6:45).

What happens to what you store in your heart?

_____

_____

_____

Now go back to the opening story about Justin. List a few of the choices Justin was making for himself.

_____

_____

_____

_____

Do you realize how many choices you, like Justin, make by yourself every day? So just like Justin, the issue is not whether you are "allowed" to make choices—you are already making choices, with or without your parents' input and approval. Wouldn't it be great to have or develop a guide that helps you know how to make right choices? Not just good choices, or better choices, but the best choices? That's our goal in this book. So let's continue looking at the nature of choices. Next comes the letter "H":

Having a plan helps you make good choices. Your choices for today started with the plans you made yesterday. When did Justin need to make his choice about setting his alarm clock?

_____

_____

_____

Think about what's happening tomorrow. Do you have a school report due? When is that big test coming? Is it tomorrow? And don't forget to ask Mom what's happening tomorrow so you can put that into your plan. List your plans for tomorrow here:

_____

_____

_____

Justin's mistakes show what can happen when you don't plan ahead. List what went wrong because Justin chose to play video games instead of getting ready for his English paper. (Don't forget what happened with his alarm clock!)

_____

_____

_____

Order your choices with God in mind. I think you can see by now, after looking at Justin's story, that your choices can have serious results. That's why you need to think about what God wants you to do. God wants to help if you will let Him. According to James 1:5, what is the best way to get the help you need to make really good choices?

If any of you lacks wisdom, you should ask of God...and it will be given to you (James 1:5).

What is the key to making right choices?.

_____

_____

What does God promise to give you when you ask Him?

_____

_____

Speaking of right or wrong, let's review. So far in Justin's story, what were Justin's wrong choices—choices you don't want to make?

_____

_____

_____

_____

Influence affects choices. What do I mean by *influence*? When someone or something affects the choices you make, *you are being influenced*.

For example: Have you ever wanted a specific pair of shoes just because your best friend got that very same pair of shoes? Or, do you watch certain TV shows just because it's cool with the other guys at school? That's influence—your choices are shaped by what other people do.

This brings us to another fact about choices: Choices are never made without influence. You may not realize it, but you are constantly being influenced in your choosing. Your family, your friends, and, let's face it, even your own fears and pride have a strong influence on what you choose to do or not do.

With so many people and outside forces bearing down upon you, it is important for you to have as many positive influences around you as possible. Otherwise, according to 1 Corinthians 15:33, what will happen when you are around the wrong kinds of people?

Do not be misled: "Bad company corrupts good character."

_____

_____

_____

Choices have one of two results. Good choices give *good* results, while bad choices give *bad* results. Justin made a choice and had fun playing his video game—and then he made another choice to not set his alarm. Those choices gave bad results: He was late for school, and he didn't finish his English paper (which he then lied about).

But often, like Justin, maybe you don't take time to think about the results of your choices. What is one thing you could tell Justin to do that would help him make better choices with better results?

_____

_____

_____

Everyone's choices are different. Ryan had asked Justin and some of the other guys to join him at a secret clubhouse. We don't know if any of the other guys' parents had a problem with Ryan's plan, but we do know Justin's parents did not want him to go. Now read this verse:

Children, obey your parents in the Lord, for this is right (Ephesians 6:1).

Why should the choices made by the other guys have no effect on Justin's choice?

_____

_____

_____

Make this your guiding principle: Your choices should agree with the standards set by God and the wishes of your parents. If you choose to do something that goes against what God or your parents want you to do, would it be a good or bad choice?

_____

Why?

_____

_____

_____

Seeking advice helps you make better choices.

Making really good choices requires you to ask for advice. The book of Proverbs repeatedly speaks about the folly of making choices without seeking the help of others. According to the following verse, what word is used to describe people who do not ask for advice? _____

> *The way of fools seems right to them, but the wise listen to advice* (Proverbs 12:15).

_____

Do you want to be wise according to the Bible's definition? If so, look at Proverbs 12:15 above and read it again. What must you do when you need to make a decision but you are not sure what choice you should make?

_____

_____

_____

☺ The Choice Is Yours ☺

Once again read the opening story of Justin's day of making choices. Here is a list of choices Justin had to make. How can you help him make better choices about these issues?

The alarm clock:

_____

_____

Telling the truth:

_____

_____

The English assignment:

_____

_____

Spending time with Ryan at the secret clubhouse:

_____

_____

🤚 Making *Really* Good Choices 🤚

In this chapter we have looked into God's Word and learned about why it is important to make really good **C-H-O-I-C-E-S.** On this page, write out the point of each letter as it was stated in your book. (I'll get you started with "C.")

Choices deal with your heart.

H_____

O_____

I_____

C_____

E_____

S_____

Now write out one thing you liked, learned, or want to do about the choices you need to make.

_____

_____

_____

_____

_____

_____

Take time now to seal your desire to make *really* good choices with the words of this prayer:

> *Choose for yourselves this day*
> *whom you will serve*
> (Joshua 24:15).

Father God, I want to thank You for all the verses in the Bible that can help me make really good choices. As Joshua 24:15 says, my most important choice each day is to "choose" to serve You. Help me make this choice today and do what Your Word says. Amen.

Choosing to Obey

When we last saw Justin Smith, he was pedaling his bike—not *toward* his home, but in the opposite direction, toward the secret clubhouse. No, Justin did not suddenly lose his sense of direction. He knew the way home. After all, he had been walking and riding this same route for the past five years. Hey, he could probably make the trip from school to home blindfolded!

So why was he going in the opposite direction?

Only one word could explain his actions—disobedience. Ouch! Justin had been clearly told by his parents not to hang out with Ryan. But still, he couldn't resist the invitation to go to the secret clubhouse after school, where some of the older boys from his neighborhood were going to do some experiments with leftover fireworks they had found in the garage of one of their homes.

Justin was extremely excited. But at the same time, he was nervous because he knew his parents' firm stand not only about Ryan, but also about playing with matches. Justin reasoned, "What's the big deal? These older guys know what they are doing. I won't actually play with the matches. *They* will! No one will know I was even there, and it will be great fun to see what happens with the fireworks."

Two hours later the clubhouse and the grassy field around it were on fire, and all the town's fire trucks had responded to keep the fire from reaching some nearby homes. When the residents described to the fire chief what had happened, they said they had seen Justin and the other boys running away from the burning field.

Fun in God's Word!

It's obvious that Justin now wishes he had listened to his parents. The consequence of his disobedience was painful in more ways than just physical! As we will see throughout this book, choices have results. Good choices have good outcomes, while bad choices, like this one Justin made, have bad results. The town will long remember that fire and the damage it caused.

It's time to look at God's Word, the Bible, and find out what God says about obedience. Grab your pen and write down your answers as we look at the following verses from the Bible. We are going to spell out O-B-E-Y.

Obey your parents. Justin made a choice to not obey his parents. What should have been his choice, according to this verse?

Children, obey your parents in the Lord, for this is right (Ephesians 6:1).

_____

_____

Here's another question: When you are not sure what the "right" thing to do is, what should you do, or who should you ask?

_____

_____

Now read Colossians 3:20.

Children, obey your parents in everything, for this pleases the Lord.

To what extent should you obey your parents, and why?

_____

_____

_____

Since this is what God wants for his guys, you should be obeying your parents "in everything." Can you think of anything you are doing now that goes against your parents' advice or rules? What do you plan to do about it?

_____

_____

_____

_____

_____

Be smart and do the right thing! Be alert. What do I mean by this? You need to be aware that bad choices don't always look like bad choices. Let's look at Justin's example again. His parents had told him not to play with matches, and probably told him the terrible things that could happen by doing so. But his friends told him how exciting it would be to see things burn, and that nothing bad would happen. They would keep things under control, and nothing would go wrong.

And here's a really big clue that should have made Justin alert. The other guys had told him, "Justin, your parents don't know what they are talking about. They sound a little old-fashioned and too strict."

Justin is not the first person who was tempted to make a bad choice. Long ago, God specifically told Adam and Eve, the first two people put on the earth, that there was something they should not do. What did God say they *could* do, according to Genesis 2:16?

> *And the* LORD *God commanded the man, "You are free to eat from any tree in the garden."*

_____

_____

_____

_____

_____

Now read verse 17:

"But you must not eat from the tree of the knowledge of good and evil, for when you eat from it you will certainly die."

What did God say Adam and Eve could *not* do? And while you are at it, go ahead and write down what God said would happen to them if they disobeyed.

_____

_____

_____

_____

Here's what happened next: The devil, disguised as a snake, came to Eve.

Now the serpent was more crafty than any of the wild animals the Lord God had made. He said to the woman, "Did God really say, 'You must not eat from any tree in the garden'?... You will not certainly die" (Genesis 3:1,4).

What did the devil say to Eve that was opposite to what God said? (See Genesis 2:16.)

_____

_____

_____

After Eve listened to the devil instead of God, she looked at her choice differently.

When the woman saw that the fruit of the tree was good for food and pleasing to the eye, and also desirable for gaining wisdom, she took some and ate it. She also gave some to her husband, who was with her, and he ate it (Genesis 3:6).

Justin and his friends almost burned down their neighborhood. But Eve and Adam's sin was even worse. Their really bad choice brought sin and death into the world.

So what have you learned from watching Justin and reading about Adam and Eve in the Bible? That it is easy to make the wrong choice even after your parents have told you, "Don't do it!" and even after you read in your Bible that God tells you, "Don't do it!" What should you do when you are tempted to not obey your parents and God? Answer: Don't do it!

Instead, be smart—and do the right thing! God says, *The son who obeys what he has been taught shows he is smart* (Proverbs 28:7 ICB™). So...

- ◎ be on your toes—when you are tempted to do something wrong.

- ◎ be suspicious—when doing something that is wrong looks like it would be fun.

- ◎ be obedient to your parents' decisions—when a choice comes up that goes against their instructions to you.

A Boy's Guide to Making Really Good Choices

Experience God's blessings. Do you like being happy? I know I sure do, and I'm guessing you do too. Well, God has said that when you obey, you will be happy. That sounds pretty good, doesn't it? And it's true. Here's what God says:

Children, obey your parents in the Lord, for this is right. "Honor your father and mother"—which is the first commandment with a promise—"so that it may go well with you and that you may enjoy long life on the earth" (Ephesians 6:1-3).

What does God tell all children to do? (List two things.)

_____

_____

When you obey your parents and honor them, what does God promise will happen, according to the last part of the passage above?

_____

_____

_____

Poor Justin. He wasn't experiencing much happiness after he disobeyed his parents. When it comes time for you to make a decision, obedience to God's ways and your parents' wishes are always the right choices. Whether it is your parents, or your teachers, or the traffic sign that says, "Do not cross here," obedience is an important key to a happy and safe life.

God has placed people, rules, and laws into your life that will help you make the right choices. Like Justin, who didn't really understand the destructive nature of fire and how quickly a spark can become a raging fire, you might not have all the information you need to make right choices. Look to God and your parents for wisdom and help.

Yield to better choices. A choice means having an option, or having several options. The nice thing about making a choice is that the decision is up to you. No one else is making you choose, so you are responsible for what happens!

Have you ever heard this little rhyme? "Good, better, best. Let your good never rest until your better becomes best." When it comes to making choices, start with making good choices. Then aim for better and best choices. Go for the best choices. They will always please God.

Let's look at two young men in the early part of the Bible named Cain and Abel. They both had a choice about what kind of offering they would bring to God. Would it be a good choice, or a better choice, or even the best choice? Take a look at what happened.

In the course of time Cain brought some of the fruits of the soil as an offering to the LORD. And Abel also brought an offering—fat portions from some of the firstborn of his flock. The LORD looked with favor on Abel and his offering, but on Cain and his offering he [God] did not look with favor (Genesis 4:3-5).

Who chose to bring the best offering to God?

_____

According to the verse below, what did Cain choose to do after his offering was rejected?

So Cain was very angry, and his face was downcast (Genesis 4:5).

_____

_____

_____

What would happen if Cain did not get control of his anger?

If you do not do what is right, sin is crouching at your door; it desires to have you, but you must rule over it (Genesis 4:8).

_____

_____

Cain did not make the right choice about his gift to God or about controlling his anger. Read on to discover what happened next.

Now Cain said to his brother Abel, "Let's go out to the field." While they were in the field, Cain attacked his brother Abel and killed him (Genesis 4:8).

What awful choice did Cain make instead of doing what was right?

_____

_____

_____

⊚ The Choice Is Yours ⊚

Wow! Did you ever imagine what could happen when you choose not to obey those in authority over you, starting with God? God tells you in His Bible exactly what is expected of you. He wants you to read your Bible and find out what are His good, better, and best choices for you and your life. When Justin went to the secret clubhouse, he didn't make the right choice. In the Garden of Eden, Adam and Eve didn't make the right choice either. Then, finally, there was Cain. God told Cain to make the right choice and warned him about the danger of making a wrong choice.

Follow what the Bible says. Obey God, and obey your parents. Then God will bless you. You will be happy, and grow up to be a man after God's own heart (Acts 13:22).

Making *Really* Good Choices

In this chapter we have looked into God's Word and learned how important it is to O-B-E-Y. On this page, write out the point of each letter. (I'll get you started with "O.")

Obey your parents.

B_____

E_____

Y_____

Now, write out one thing you liked, learned, or want to do about obeying.

_____

_____

_____

_____

_____

_____

 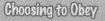

Take time now to seal your desire to make *really* good choices with the words of this prayer:

Dear God, help me to take more time with my choices. I want to learn to wait and talk to my parents and find out what You say about my choices. Give me the courage to say, "No" when I am asked to do something I know is wrong. I want to do what You want me to do. Amen.

Choosing to Get Up

Poor Justin! He's really having a terrible day, isn't he? And it all started the night before when he chose to stay up and play an electronic game. Sure, he had some great fun, but now he's about to have a rude awakening. Can you picture the scene—and the sound? Justin is in a deep, dead sleep. Totally knocked out! And then there was a terrible noise. It took a while for Justin to realize what that sound was—it was his mom speaking to him with her voice raised just loud enough to make him realize he was in big trouble.

Have you been there and done that? Done what Justin did? Gotten into trouble by making poor choices? That's the way bad choices go, isn't it? It's like playing dominoes.

As a young boy I often sat beside my dad as he played dominoes with other adult family members. When our dads took a break, I and all of my cousins would play with the dominoes by standing them on end in a long line.

This would go on until one of us had a shaky hand or bumped the table. Then the dominoes would rapidly topple one by one—each one tipping the next one over...tipping the next one over...tipping the next one over...until all the dominoes had fallen. That tumbling of all the dominoes is called "the domino effect."

When it comes to you and your choices, a good choice leads to good things. But one poor or bad or wrong choice starts a chain reaction that creates trouble and usually ends badly.

It is obvious that Justin wishes he had made a better choice about going to bed. And, as we work our way through this book about your life and your choices, you will see this one singular choice—getting up on time—will start your day right and make a difference in the quality of your whole day. You'll see how Choice #1 (getting up), affects Choice #2...and #3...and #4. It's like the domino effect.

Fun in God's Word!

But never fear—help is on the way! It's time again to look at God's Word, the Bible, and find out what God says about getting to bed...and getting up. Have you got a pen handy? You will want to write down a few answers as you look at some verses from the Bible. We are going to spell out G-E-T-U-P.

God's Word talks about being lazy. The Bible has a lot to say about a person who is lazy, calling such a person a "sluggard," or someone who has a bad habit of not wanting to get out of bed, or is slow in everything they do, or is content to goof off all the time. A sluggard is anyone who hates to get up and hates to work. It's also someone who moves slowly out of laziness—much like the way a giant slug moves slowly across a sidewalk or driveway. Now read Proverbs 6:9-10, and write out the questions that are asked in the two verses:

How long will you lie there, you sluggard? When will you get up from your sleep? A little sleep, a little slumber, a little folding of the hands to rest—and poverty [ruin] *will come on you like a thief* (Proverbs 6:9-11).

Question#1: _____

_____

Question #2: _____

_____

What happens to a sluggard who wants to sleep?

_____

_____

A sluggard does not even know that he is in trouble, as his ruin comes upon him like a _____.

God often uses word pictures to describe truth. Read the next verse, then write out God's description of a door as it turns on its hinges:

As a door turns on its hinges, so a sluggard turns on his bed (Proverbs 26:14).

What does a door do?

_____

_____

What does a sluggard (or a boy who won't get up) do?

_____

_____

Evaluate the advantage of getting up. To _evaluate_
means to look closely at something. So let's take a closer
look at a few men in the Bible and see how they started off
their days with some key choices. As you go through this section, feel free to mark up and interact with the verses. These
guys have an important message for you!

Abraham was a great man of God in the Old Testament.
He worshipped God, served God, and lived for God. In the
Bible, we learn that God wanted to destroy several cities that
were filled with evil people. What did Abraham do? He asked
God to please save the good people who lived in the wicked
cities of Sodom and Gomorrah. What did Abraham do the
very next day so he could find out what God would do?

> _Early the next morning Abraham got up and returned to the
> place where he had stood before the_ LORD (Genesis 19:27).

Note the time: _____

_____

Note the place: _____

_____

You too can talk to God through prayer. Getting up early to spend some time with God is a great way to start your day. It's also a *really* good choice!

Jesus also teaches us about this important habit in His own life. Read the verse below.

Very early in the morning, while it was still dark, Jesus got up, left the house and went off to a solitary place, where he prayed (Mark 1:35).

Note the time: _____

_____

Note the place: _____

_____

Note the purpose: _____

_____

Jesus talked to His heavenly Father first thing in the morning. He prayed to God about His life and His day. How did praying early in the day help Jesus? It gave Him strength and wisdom for doing God's will. Getting up and spending time with God can arm you too for facing and dealing with all kinds of temptation like the ones we are discussing in this book—the temptation to lie, to disobey, to be mean.

List two things you can do to help you get up tomorrow morning when you should.

1._____

_____

2._____

_____

David is another man in the Bible who knew how important it was to get up on time each day. David was a mighty warrior who became a mighty king. Here's what he wrote:

In the morning, LORD, you hear my voice; in the morning I lay my requests before you and wait expectantly (Psalm 5:3).

Note the time: _____

_____

Note David's purpose: _____

_____

David spent time in the morning to talk over his day and his problems and concerns with God. What is facing you today? Tomorrow? Do you have a test? Do you have to give a book review? Is your team or group competing or performing? Do you have to go to the dentist? Jot down what's going on. According to David and Abraham and Jesus, what should you do about it?

_____

_____

Teens who get up. What young guy your age doesn't want to be a teen? How old are you now, and how long do you have to wait to wear the label *teenager*? Do you ever wonder if your thirteenth birthday will *ever* come? Well, don't worry—it will!

So far we've talked about the bad habits of being a sluggard and lazy. Well, you can start right now to develop the great habit of getting up early or on time. And there are lots of teens who already know the benefits of doing that.

For instance, did you get to watch the gymnastics and swim competitions during the last Olympics? Many of those athletes were already well on their way to being the best in their sport when they were your age. They trained for years to get to the place where they could perform in the worldwide Olympics. They had to get up early to train at the gym or swimming pool to become great at what they do. Most of them spend one or two hours in practice *before* they go to school, and then again after school.

And what about the boys who do well in football, or soccer, or baseball at the local middle school and high school? How did these teens get to be good enough to play on their teams? They learned to get up early and stay up late to do their studies, do their chores, and fulfill their responsibilities so they could have the time both before and after school to train for these sports.

What is it you are passionate about? What is it you love doing more than anything else? What is it you would like to do but never seem to have enough time for? Take a minute to jot down an answer or two.

I like to, or I would really like to...

_____

_____

_____

_____

Understand the importance of getting up. Are you looking for a good day with time for not only the necessary stuff, but also for some fun too? Then there is one *really simple* but *really hard* choice you've got to make every day. In fact, it is the *first* choice, the right choice, you must make each morning, whether you realize it or not. That choice is, will you get up when you need to...or not? Read what this Bible verse says:

Everything should be done in a fitting and orderly way (1 Corinthians 14:40).

What two qualities mark a job well done?

1._____

2._____

This verse is a great reminder to do all things well, in the right way—not in a hurry, not sloppy, not taking shortcuts, not seeing how little you can get by with, not doing a job poorly just to get it done.

When you get up early or at the time you need to, you will have time to do things right. I hate to say it, but when you don't get outta that bed when you're supposed to so you can get everything done "in a proper and orderly way," the domino effect goes into action and *every*thing suffers for the rest of the day. It's amazing how that one first really good choice influences everything else.

Purpose to get up. As you think about living your life God's way, let the following choices guide you toward your goal. This exercise will help you follow through on your first step toward a better life—getting out of bed!

Step 1: Decide with your parents when you should get up.
(And be prepared for their shock! Your parents might not believe their ears when you ask for their help on this one.)

Step 2: Determine when you must get up to make your day go the way you wish it to go.

Step 3. Set your alarm...a good *loud* one. An obnoxious one!

Step 4: Get to bed in time to get the rest you need before getting-up time. (No playing electronic games all night long under the bedcovers!)

Step 5: Pray. Ask for God's help to get up at the right time. Tell Him why it is important that you get up. Go over your plans, purpose, commitments, and dreams for tomorrow with Him. Go ahead. He cares!

Step 6: Purpose to get up...no matter what. Don't give in to the temptation to sleep longer. And don't worry about not getting enough sleep for that day. It's only for *one* morning!

Step 7: Praise God when you hear the alarm. Think in your heart these words from Psalm 118:24: *This is the day which the LORD has made; let us rejoice and be glad in it* (NASB).

☺ The Choice Is Yours ☺

Life is a precious gift from God. On top of the life He has given you, He also has incredible plans and purposes for you as well. Nothing could be worse than a life that counts for nothing. You have all the opportunities in the world to make a difference, contribute to others, and honor God.

Each morning when your sleep is shattered by the alarm clock, realize that it is right then and right there that you make maybe *the* most important choice you will make all day. It goes like this: If you get up, you are in control of yourself and your day. (Well, at least you're in control of how it begins!) From the very first minute—Minute #1—you are calling the shots. You are in the driver's seat of your day when you make a choice to get up. Don't be like the sluggard:

Photo of a "Sluggard"
1. A sluggard will not begin things.
2. A sluggard will not finish things.
3. A sluggard will not face things.[1]

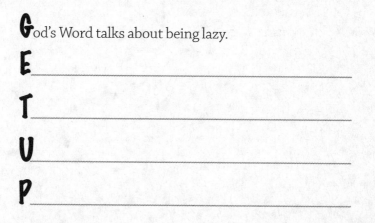 Making *Really* Good Choices

In this chapter we have looked into God's Word and learned how important it is to G-E-T-U-P. On this page, write out the point of each letter. (I'll get you started with "G.")

God's Word talks about being lazy.

E _____

T _____

U _____

P _____

Now write out one thing you liked, learned, or want to do about getting up.

_____

_____

_____

_____

_____

Take time now to seal your desire to make *really* good choices with the words of this prayer:

Dear Jesus, I think I'm a little like that sluggard, but I want to change. I want to make the right choice tomorrow morning to get up when I'm supposed to. Thank You for all the Bible verses that show me how important this choice is. Amen.

Choosing to Read Your Bible

It is now well past time for Justin to be getting ready for school. Remember, we left him scurrying around trying to get ready for school because he had been too lazy to set his alarm clock the night before. His mother finally had to barge into his room with a very irritated look and ask, "Justin, why aren't you up and dressed?"

Busted! Quickly Justin tells himself, *Think fast!* as he wipes the sleep from his eyes. With a plan in mind, he blurts out, "There must be something wrong with my alarm clock! It didn't go off." (Yeah, that's it. I'll blame it on the alarm clock!) "Mom, you need to buy me a new one." Then, for his final defense, Jason shouts out, "Why didn't you wake me, Mom? You knew I have a big day at school!"

With this, Justin's mother raises her hands as a sign of hopelessness and walks out of the room.

Whew, thought Justin, *that was a close one.* As he staggers out of bed, he notices his Bible lying on the nightstand and the study book the guys in his Sunday school class were going through. "Oh no! I didn't finish today's lesson. And Mr. Howard said we should do one a day to get into the habit of reading God's Word every day."

Justin sighs, "Oh well, no big deal. Right now I've got more important things to deal with. I'm late for school! Maybe I can finish my Bible lesson during history class. Mr. Brown is soooo boring!"

Fun in God's Word!

Life is a gift from God. On top of the life He has given you, He also has incredible plans and purposes for you as well. You've heard this before, but here it is again: Nothing could be worse than a life that counts for nothing. You have all of the opportunities in the world to live an exciting life, to make a difference, to help others, and to live for God.

So be like an Army Ranger or a Navy SEAL who stands before his commanding officer—his CO—each day, ready to receive his orders. You need orders, purpose, and direction. Are you ready to receive your marching orders from God? Here's how:

Each morning when your sleep is shattered like Justin's was, realize that it is right then and right there that you make what may be *the* most important choice you will make all day. It goes like this. If you get up right away, you are in control of yourself and your day. (Well, at least you're in control of how it begins! You have to leave room for God's plans, for interruptions, even crises.) Why can I say that? Because from Minute #1, you are calling the shots. You are in the driver's seat of your day, so to speak, when you make a choice to get up immediately!

And now it is time for another *really* good choice: *Choosing to read your Bible*—to have a quiet time. This is where your CO—God Himself—"speaks" to you and gives you the marching orders for your day. This step will *really* set the tone of your day, and your voice, and your words, and your actions, and your attitudes, and the way you treat people— starting right at home! So once you are up, you want to make God your #1 priority. You want to choose to put first things first. You want to meet with Him first thing, before the day gets rolling.

It is time again to look at God's Word, the Bible, and find out what God says about choosing to read your Bible. And it's time to get a pen for writing down your answers as we look up some verses. We are going to spell out B-I-B-L-E.

Bible reading is a must. Anything that is a priority must be seen as important, something you put at the top of your to-do list. Why is reading the Bible to be a priority? Because that is where you find out more about God, who should be your #1 priority. Right?

A great place to start learning about God is Genesis 1:1:

In the beginning God created the heavens and the earth.

This is the very first verse of the Bible. What does it tell you about God?

_____

_____

After you get out of bed, you want to make the really good choice to spend time in the Bible. It's a key time for learning about God, who created you and everything around you.

Important answers come from the Bible. I'm sure that at your age, you are beginning to have a lot of questions about life. Read the questions below and check the ones you would like to have answered.

_____ Are you wondering about your future?

_____ Are you looking for a few good friends?

_____ Are you tired of doing the wrong thing?

_____ Would you like to get along better with your parents?

Well, I've got great news for you! Time in God's Word will help you to have success in every one of these areas—and more. We learn this from looking at a man in the Bible whose name is Joshua. He was the man who took Moses' place when Moses died, and he became the general of God's army.

Like every general and leader, Joshua wondered if he would be successful in the battle to win the Promised Land for God's people. Read the verse below and write out the command God gave Joshua to guarantee his success.

Be careful to obey all the law [the Bible] *my servant Moses gave you...that you may be successful wherever you go* (Joshua 1:7).

_____

_____

_____

_____

Now read the next verse and write out the two things God told Joshua to do to make sure he would be successful in God's eyes.

Keep this Book of the Law always on your lips; meditate on it day and night...Then you will be prosperous and success-ful (Joshua 1:8).

1._____

_____

2._____

_____

God wants to bless you and help you have success. Are you wondering what you can do to help make this success happen? Here are a few steps you can take each day that will help you choose God as a top priority—actually, your #1 priority!

Step 1: Read your Bible. I could say, "Just read it!" Start anywhere you like. You could even start with the book of Joshua! The only wrong way to read the Bible is not to read the Bible.

Step 2: Study your Bible. Ask your parents or youth leader to help you find some simple ways to get to know your Bible better.

Step 3: Hear the Bible taught. Make sure you go to your youth group meetings and church to hear God's Word taught and explained so you can understand it—and, of course, choose to do what it says.

Step 4: Memorize verses from the Bible. God told Joshua to "meditate" on the Bible. That means to think about God's Word a lot so it is always in your heart.

Step 5: Desire to spend time in God's Word. You already know the importance of eating physical food. Well, you need to see the spiritual food the Bible gives you as being important too...only more so! As Job declared, *I have treasured the words of his mouth* [God's teaching] *more than my daily bread* (Job 23:12).

Bible truths give you direction. Have you ever gotten lost temporarily in a shopping mall or large store? You looked around and couldn't see your mom or dad or big sister or brother. Being lost is a scary experience. Well, wouldn't it be nice to always know where you are going and never get lost? How is the Bible described in this verse?

Your word [the Bible] *is a lamp for my feet, and a light on my path* (Psalm 119:105).

1. The Bible is _____

_____

2. The Bible is _____

_____

The Bible is like a flashlight that shows you the path your life *should* take—the path God wants you to take. Without that light you could easy stumble and fall—or go down the wrong path spiritually!

As you read the verse that follows, what is a very important goal you should have for your life?

How can a young man stay on the path of purity? (Psalm 119:9).

_____

_____

Read the second part of Psalm 119:9. Here God gives you the answer to the question above. Be sure to write out the answer!

By living according to your word [the Bible].

_____

_____

_____

Are you ready for another cool verse about God and His Word? Read on!

All Scripture [the Bible] *is God-breathed and is useful for teaching, rebuking, correcting and training in righteousness* (2 Timothy 3:16).

What two truths do you learn about the Bible?

1. The Bible is _____

_____

2. The Bible is _____

_____

Look again at the verse above, 2 Timothy 3:16. Then fill in the blanks below to make a list of the four things the Bible will do to you as you read it:

1. The Bible will_____ me.

2. The Bible will_____ me.

3. The Bible will_____ me.

4. The Bible will_____ me.

Is there any one thing from 2 Timothy 3:16 that stands out to you? Is there something you want to pay more attention to each day? Circle what challenges you.

Life changes come from the Bible. Like all boys, you are looking forward to being a teenager so you can do more fun things, right? Well, while you are waiting for your thirteenth birthday, you can start making changes to prepare you for those years.

Read the verses below from Psalm 19:7-11 to see what meeting with God in the Bible can do to get you ready for your day—and your life! *Circle* the words that describe God's Word. Then *underline* the effect it has on those who read it. I'll guide you through the first example. Then you can do the rest yourself.

Psalm 19:7: *The law of the LORD is perfect* [circle the word "perfect"], *refreshing the soul* [underline these words].

Now try it yourself!

The statutes of the LORD are trustworthy, making wise the simple.

Psalm 19:8: *The precepts of the LORD are right, giving joy to the heart.*

The commands of the LORD are radiant, giving light to the eyes.

In Psalm 19:10, underline how valuable God's Word should be to you.

They are more precious than gold, than much pure gold.

They are sweeter than honey, than honey from the honey-comb.

In Psalm 19:11, write out the two benefits you experience as you listen to God's Word—and obey it.

By them your servant is warned;
in keeping them there is great reward.

_____

_____

_____

_____

Eternal life is found in the Bible. I once read a book about the adventures of Ponce de León, who went searching for what was called the Fountain of Youth. He thought if he could find this fountain and drink some of its water, it would give him eternal youth, eternal life. He would be forever young, and live forever.

You probably don't want to think about staying young forever. But you would probably like to live forever, right? The Bible tells us how that is possible—how you can live forever with Jesus in heaven.

There was a young man in the Bible who wanted to know how to live with Jesus forever. His name was Timothy. Read what 2 Timothy 3:15 says.

The Holy Scriptures [the Bible]...*are able to make you wise for salvation through faith in Jesus Christ.*

What book gave Timothy the wisdom he needed for salvation—for a relationship with Jesus? For eternal life?

_____

_____

Also, according to this verse, how do we receive salvation?

_____

_____

Do you want to live with Jesus in heaven and have eternal life? I'm thinking you do! Well, God wants to give you eternal life, but there is just one problem: You need to be perfect, without sin.

Yes, you already know you don't always make the right choices, which leads to doing right things. Therefore, you need a Savior. Jesus is perfect. He is God. He came to earth to die for your sins and be your Savior.

Choose to believe in Jesus, God's Son. He will give you eternal life.

☺ The Choice Is Yours ☺

Sometimes you may think you are just too busy to stop and spend time with God. I mean, you have people to see, places to go, and things to do! But it's wrong when you choose to think this way. God is more important than anything else in our life. And, as we have seen, His Word, the Bible, is a special book. In fact, it's the greatest book ever written. It's the book that can show you the right way and lead you to eternal life.

And if you are a Christian—if you have believed in Jesus and received Him into your heart as your Savior—you have that eternal life. As a Christian, you have God's Spirit in you—the Holy Spirit. He will help guide you as you read God's Word. That's why it is so important for you to choose to spend time reading the Bible. When you read it, you will think differently. You will live differently. You will grow spiritually. And you will be blessed.

Don't you think these blessings are worth the choice to get up a few minutes earlier each day so you can get into God's Word and get your marching orders for the day ahead? Through the Bible, God will tell you what really good choices you need to make. He will show you how to live your life His way.

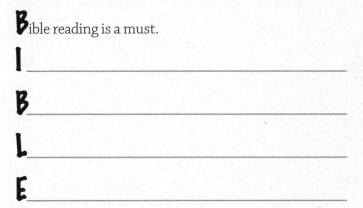 Making *Really* Good Choices

In this chapter you have looked into God's Word and learned how important it is to read your B-I-B-L-E. On this page, write out the point of each letter. (I'll get you started with "B.")

Bible reading is a must.

I_____

B_____

L_____

E_____

Now write out one thing you liked, learned, or want to do about getting up and getting into God's Word, the Bible.

_____

_____

_____

_____

_____

Take time now to seal your desire to make *really* good choices with the words of this prayer:

Hear my prayer, Father. Thank You that Your Word tells me how to live my life and make really good choices. And thank You most of all that the Bible shows me Your Son and how He wants me to live for Him here on earth and with Him forever in heaven. Amen.

Choosing to Pray

Hallelujah! Justin is finally awake! Whew!

Well, his triumph lasts for only a few seconds. Why? Because, as he stands by his bed staring at his Bible and his unfinished Bible study lesson on the nightstand, it occurs to him that he has forgotten his commitment to pray every day this week. He had not really wanted to make the commitment to pray daily, but most of the boys in his Sunday school class had wanted to take up their teacher's challenge to pray every day this week. Mr. Howard was teaching the boys about prayer and wanted the guys to put their learning into practice by making a pledge to pray.

Still in a sleepy daze, Justin mutters to himself, "What was I thinking? I can't believe I did that! What a waste of time. Everything is going great in my life. So why do I need to pray? And for who...and what? Am I supposed to pray for missionaries I don't even know? For sick people I hardly know? And, yeah, family's important, but I'm not so sure about praying for Jake and Sally. Even though they're my brother and sister, they are such a pain!

"Oh well...okay God. Here goes. 'Please bless the missionaries and my family today, even Jake and Sally (ugh!)—and of course, bless me! Amen.'

"Now, I wonder what's for breakfast today!"

Fun in God's Word!

Did you know that the Bible is filled with information about prayer? From cover to cover—from Genesis to Revelation—the men who believed in God prayed to God. They prayed when there was trouble. They prayed when they worshipped. They prayed for people. They prayed while in battle. Whenever they needed strength, or needed to make a decision—to make a really good choice—they turned to God and talked their situation over with Him.

And then there is the example of Jesus and the many times the Bible shows Him praying to God, His heavenly Father. I don't know about you, but in my mind I'm thinking, *If Jesus, who was God Himself, needed and wanted to talk to God, how much more do I need to do the same?!*

Prayer is sort of like being on a team. For instance, you are involved in the sport or project as a team, but there is a team leader, or captain, or coach, or conductor. Someone is the leader. That leader is someone you can look to for help, listen to for advice, and follow because of that person's experience and knowledge.

Let's read a few tips the Bible gives us about talking things over with God, your spiritual leader, through prayer. When you are done, you will have spelled out P-R-A-Y-E-R. Is your pen in hand?

Prayer is talking to God. You probably have no problem talking with your friends, do you? Justin and his best friend, Matt, could talk about baseball...or soccer...or their latest video game for hours—and they do! But the thought of talking to someone outside your circle? Forget it—no way!

It is the same way when it comes to talking to God. When your relationship with God is not a close one, you will find it harder to talk to Him. You won't know what to say, and you won't feel close enough to Him to be comfortable in His presence. What's the solution? Write out the advice these verses give you.

Draw near to God with a sincere heart (Hebrews 10:22).

What is it *you* are to do?

_____

_____

What should your heart attitude be when you pray?

_____

_____

Come near to God and he will come near to you (James 4:8).

What is your role in prayer?

_____

_____

_____

What is God's response?

_____

_____

_____

Be sure to notice that these verses tell you it is your responsibility to move toward God. If God feels like a stranger to you, remember, it is *you* who has moved away from God. God did not move away from you.

Try this exercise for one week. Each day just talk to God. "Draw near" and "come near" to Him. Then use your pen or pencil to color in the box. Tell God about your worries, questions, and problems. You'll be glad you did. And, of course, you will want to keep doing this day after day.

Today I Talked to God in Prayer						
Mon.	Tues.	Wed.	Thurs.	Fri.	Sat.	Sun.

Realize how important prayer is. Another reason we don't pray is because we don't really believe in the power of prayer. That is Justin's problem. Like Justin, we say, "What difference does it make?" We think this way because we don't know about the many awesome promises God makes in the Bible about prayer and about answering our prayers. As a result, we don't think prayer makes any difference. So...we don't pray.

What does the Bible say about how you should pray? Read on and jot down some answers. Learn all you can about prayer, about talking things over with God.

Let us then approach God's throne of grace with confidence, so that we may receive mercy and find grace to help us in our time of need (Hebrews 4:16).

What is your job in prayer?

_____

_____

_____

What does God give you when you pray?

_____

_____

_____

Whatever you ask for in prayer, believe that you have received it, and it will be yours (Mark 11:24).

What is your job or part in prayer?

1._____

_____

2._____

_____

What does Mark 11:24 say happens as a result?

_____

_____

Think about it: Does this mean that you can ask and get anything you want, like a new bike or skateboard or an electronic game? For help with the answer, look at the next verse:

> *When you ask, you do not receive, because you ask with wrong motives, that you may spend what you get on your pleasures* (James 4:3).

What is one huge reason you don't always get what you ask for from God? Underline your answer in the verse above.

Assurances and promises about prayer. It is a fact: We are often clueless about how prayer works. And we don't understand how it helps us or fits into our relationship with God and making really good choices. It is probably because we don't really understand God's love for us and His power to make our lives better.

As you read the Bible verses below, write from each verse what God is promising to you when you pray:

> *Ask and it will be given to you; seek and you will find; knock and the door will be opened to you* (Matthew 7:7).

God's promise to me is

_____

_____

_____

Call to me and I will answer you and tell you great and unsearchable things you do not know (Jeremiah 33:3).

God's promise to me is

_____

_____

_____

If any of you lacks wisdom, you should ask God...and it will be given to you (James 1:5).

God's promise to me is

_____

_____

_____

You need to confess sin before you pray. Here is another big reason we don't pray: It is because we have done something wrong. In our hearts we know we need to talk to God about it. We know we need to confess it, to agree with Him that what we did was wrong. Let's look at a few verses that talk about confessing your sin.

If I regard [sin] *in my heart, the LORD will not hear* (Psalm 66:18 NKJV).

What happens when you sin and don't confess it to God?

_____

_____

_____

If we confess our sins, he is faithful and just and will forgive us our sins and purify us from all unrighteousness (1 John 1:9).

What happens when you confess your sin and admit it to God?

_____

_____

_____

Here's a good exercise for dealing with your sins and failures: Make a choice to keep short accounts with God. This means you deal with any sin as it comes up—on the spot—at the exact minute that you slip up and fail. Say,

"Lord, I'm sorry for _____.

Thank You for forgiving me in Jesus."

Examples of people who prayed. The Bible is filled with people who made the really good choice to pray about their life and their choices. See what you can learn about the difference that prayer made in these people's lives. Also, pay attention to what they talked to God about.

King David praised God in prayer—David faced many trials, enemies, problems, and hard situations. He wrote these words:

> *I will exalt you, O LORD, for you lifted me out of the depths and did not let my enemies gloat over me. LORD my God, I called to you for help, and you healed me* (Psalm 30:1-2).

It is no wonder that David praised God! After he prayed to God, what did God do?

_____

_____

_____

Abraham prayed for his family—Abraham's family was living in another area. He could not talk to them and help them, but he could talk to God about them and pray for their safety (Genesis 18:20-33).

Who in your family at home needs prayer this week, and for what?

_____

_____

_____

What family members are not at home and need your prayers this week? And for what?

_____

_____

_____

Jesus—Wow! Jesus was perfect and knew everything about prayer. Read these Bible verses that describe some of the times He prayed:

Mark 1:35: *Very early in the morning, while it was still dark, Jesus got up, left the house and went off to a solitary place where he prayed.*

John 6:11: *Jesus then took the loaves, gave thanks, and distributed to those who were seated...He did the same with the fish.*

Matthew 26:39: [Before going to the cross, Jesus] *fell with his face to the ground and prayed, "My Father, if it is possible, may this cup be taken from me. Yet not as I will, but as you will."*

Luke 23:34: [On the cross] *Jesus said, "Father, forgive them, for they do not know what they are doing."*

After looking at these verses, what one lesson have you learned from Jesus about prayer?

_____

_____

Realize that God is always available to you. Have you ever noticed that your parents' cell phones are always on and available? This means people can call them at all hours of the day or night.

Your prayer life is like a cell phone—you can pray anytime you want, anywhere you are, and talk to God for as long as you want. You have a direct line to the God of the universe 24/7—24 hours a day, 7 days a week. How's that for immediate access to God? Notice what the following verse says about God's availability.

The LORD is near to all who call on him, to all who call on him in truth (Psalm 145:18).

What do you learn about God in this verse?

_____

_____

_____

What is it you are to do?

_____

_____

_____

☺ The Choice Is Yours ☺

There are many excuses you can give about why you choose not to pray. You can be like Justin, who chose not to take the time or make an effort to pray. Prayer was not a priority for him. It was not important. Instead, Justin filled his time with things that he wanted to do—things he thought were more important.

The choice is yours. You can choose to be like Justin and be so busy you don't even get around to *thinking* about praying. But I'm guessing you probably are like most guys and simply haven't made the effort to talk to God. Prayer is an act of the will. It is a choice. You have to *want* to do it... and choose to do it. The choice is yours.

🖐 Making *Really* Good Choices 🖐

In this chapter we have looked into God's Word and learned the importance of P-R-A-Y-E-R. On this page, write out the point of each letter. (I'll get you started with "P.")

Prayer is talking to God.

R _____

A _____

Y _____

E _____

R _____

Now write out one thing you liked, learned, or want to do about making prayer an important part of your life.

_____

_____

_____

_____

_____

Take time now to seal your desire to make *really* good choices with the words of this prayer:

Lord, I want to talk things over with You. I know I need Your help. Thank You that whenever I call out to You, You are there to listen and guide me to make the right choices. Amen.

Choosing Your Friends

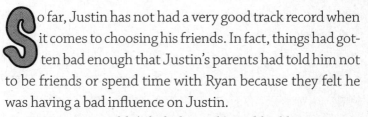

So far, Justin has not had a very good track record when it comes to choosing his friends. In fact, things had gotten bad enough that Justin's parents had told him not to be friends or spend time with Ryan because they felt he was having a bad influence on Justin.

But Justin couldn't help himself. He liked hanging out with Ryan. Ryan was older, and his parents bought him all sorts of great video games. His house had just about every cool electronics device you could think of. Plus, Ryan had his own TV in his room and even a DVD player and recorder. And, of course, Ryan had a computer with Internet access and no parental restrictions! Ryan often told Justin about some of the things he discovered as he was surfing the Net.

Sure, Justin was a little uneasy with some of what Ryan talked about. But the temptation of the unknown was drawing Justin into a harmful friendship with Ryan. Then came that awful field fire caused by the fireworks. Yes, Ryan was one of the older boys who had been playing with the forbidden fireworks!

Now we find Justin at school, slowly making his way through the crowded halls. He is headed to his locker to get his books before the start of his first class. And, once again, he is about to go down that same familiar trail of choosing the wrong kind of friends as he sees Ted. Meet Ted, whose locker is next to Justin's. Justin and Ted have been friends for years. They are also both members of his boys' class at church.

But for some reason, Justin has started drifting away from Ted and their longtime friendship. You see, because Justin was now hanging out with Ryan and his friends, Justin had decided he didn't want to spend as much time with Ted and the other church kids who just weren't that popular. And they always seemed out of place. They dressed a little differently and acted differently in an uncool way. At least that's what Ryan had told Justin. Ryan even called them "religious weirdos."

So Justin gave Ted a half smile and then grabbed his books.

"See ya on Sunday?" Ted called as Justin quickly headed for class.

Justin liked Ted and the others from church. In fact, he wished he could be as strong as Ted. But he didn't like being seen as different. He especially wanted to be liked by the "in crowd" at school.

And speaking of the popular kids, here comes another one of Ryan's friends. "See ya," Justin mumbled to Ted as he turned to join his new friend.

Fun in God's Word!

You may be one of those guys who never meets a stranger. I mean, you can talk to anybody about anything! Making friends is no problem at all. Or maybe you are a guy who has a longtime friend like Justin had in Ted, and the two of you are inseparable. But for most guys, it is not easy to find a good friend.

Well, God comes to the rescue for us. He tells us exactly what kinds of friends to have—and what kinds *not* to have. So let's begin our discussion about friendships by taking a look at God's Word, the Bible. We need to find out what God says about the very important choice of choosing friends, and not just any friends, but the right kind. So once again, get yourself a pen and write down your answers as we look at some verses from the Bible. In this chapter, we are going to spell out F-R-I-E-N-D-S.

Finding a friend takes time. Did you know that if you are a Christian you already have a very special friend in Jesus? Jesus said to His disciples: *You are my friends...I have called you friends* (John 15:14-15). With Jesus as your friend, you have the very best friend a person could have. You can talk to Him through prayer at any time and in any situation. And best of all, He is always with you. What do these two verses tell you about your friend, Jesus?

Surely I am with you always, to the very end of the age (Matthew 28:20).

_____

_____

Never will I leave you; never will I forsake you (Hebrews 13:5).

_____

_____

This is awesome news! Jesus is always with you and available to you. And God also provides others who can and should be your friends. For instance:

You have friends in your parents. Now before you wonder how that is possible, realize that there is nothing weird about having your mom and dad as friends. In fact, they are God's gift to you. And no one loves you more or cares about you more than your parents do. Ask God to help you to develop a lasting friendship with your parents...starting now.

You also have friends in your brothers and sisters. You are probably thinking, *Are you kidding? Friends with my goofy brother? No way!* Or, *Friends with my little sister? Ick! What a pest!*
   Believe it or not, your friends throughout life will come and go. You might stay in touch with some, but eventually most of your friends will move on. But your family will always be there, no matter what...or where. And here's some good news: As you and your brother and sister get older, you will all get along better.

Reject certain people as friends. The Bible is very clear when it speaks to you of what kind of person to look for in a friend—and what kind to avoid! Let's look at a list of people God tells you to reject as friends. As you read through these verses, make a note about the speech, character, or conduct of those who are *not* to be your friends and the *effect* they can have on you.

Walk with the wise and become wise, for a companion of fools suffers harm (Proverbs 13:20).

_____

_____

_____

Do not make friends with a hot-tempered person, do not associate with one easily angered (Proverbs 22:24).

_____

_____

_____

Do not be misled: "Bad company corrupts good character" (1 Corinthians 15:33).

_____

_____

_____

Involve your parents. Now why would you want to choose to include or listen to your mom and dad when it comes to your friendships? How could your parents possibly be helpful in your quest to find friends?

First, your parents have a little more experience in finding friends than you have. So, trust me, they can be a great help!

And besides, according to God's plan in Ephesians 6:1 (*Children, obey your parents in the Lord, for this is right*), they are the final authority on who you do and don't welcome as friends.

Take Justin, for example. Justin wanted to be friends with Ryan not because Ryan was a good and godly influence on him, but because Ryan had cool things and knew stuff! Justin's parents could see how Ryan was influencing Justin in a bad way, which Justin did not see—or didn't want to see.

Talk to your parents about what kinds of friends and friendships you should have. And be sure your new friends come to your house and meet your parents.

Here's another "friendship" verse:

What does 2 Timothy 2:22 say you are to do as a youth or tween boy?

Flee the evil desires of youth...

_____

_____

_____

Instead you are to do what?

...and pursue righteousness, faith, love and peace...

_____

_____

_____

What kinds of friends will want to join you on your journey to becoming a boy, teen, and man after God's own heart?

...along with those who call on the Lord out of a pure heart.

_____

_____

_____

Once again, what does the Bible say you should do if your parents say *no* to certain guys as your friends?

Children, obey your parents in the Lord, for this is right (Ephesians 6:1).

_____

_____

_____

Encourage your friends. Have you ever thought about how easy it is to tell other kids all the things you think they are doing wrong? They are wearing the wrong clothes, or talking funny, or acting goofy or the wrong way. Instead of discouraging others, however, what does the Bible say you are to do, and what happens when you do it?

Encourage one another and build each other up (1 Thessalonians 5:11).

_____

_____

_____

Make it a habit to mention the good qualities and attitudes you see in others.

What is the best way to be an encourager? Well, the Bible tells us how David encouraged his best friend, Jonathan. Their relationship was based on their mutual love for God. When Jonathan's father, King Saul, wanted to kill David, what did Jonathan do to encourage David?

Saul's son Jonathan went to David at Horesh and helped him find strength in God (1 Samuel 23:16).

_____

_____

_____

The best way to encourage your friends is to help them "find strength in God" through the Bible and through prayer. And you can say kind words to them. Praise them not for their cool clothes or things, but for something you appreciate about them, something you admire about their conduct or their character. For example, is your friend honest? Is he committed to the team and faithful? Is he kind and helpful to his little brother or sister? Tell him. When you build up another person instead of tearing him down, you help him grow and develop in a good way.

Nice is always in. Have you ever heard of the Golden Rule? And did you know that Jesus taught this rule? Write out what Jesus says you are to do to others.

Do to others as you would have them do to you (Luke 6:31).

_____

_____

Here's an exercise: List three or four ways you want others to treat you:

_____

_____

_____

_____

Now, according to the Golden Rule, how should you be treating others?

_____

_____

_____

_____

And remember, the Golden Rule doesn't just say to be nice. Read the next verse. Instead of just being "nice," what does the Bible say you are to do?

Be kind and compassionate to one another (Ephesians 4:32).

_____

_____

_____

_____

Here's a bonus question: The Golden Rule begins at home, because the person you are at home is the person you really are. Write down one way you will practice the Golden Rule with your parents and brothers and sisters.

_____

_____

_____

Decide to be yourself. Don't try to impress others by saying and doing things you think will make them like you. It's tempting to act in a way that goes against God's Word to get friends or be accepted by the "in crowd." You are looking for friends who aren't phony—who don't pretend to be a certain kind of person when they are not. For yourself, you should want to be the real thing, to be what God desires you to be—a godly young man. So be that person, even if it means you won't be the most popular guy at school. At least you will be *you*. You will be genuine. And God will be pleased with you.

Spiritual maturity is important. So choose to be growing spiritually. This is always the first choice you must make in every area of your life, and friendships are no different. If you desire to grow spiritually and know more about God and how He wants you to act, you will want friends who share your desire to grow.

Take a look at the young man Daniel, who had three really good young friends who stood with him. Their names were Shadrach, Meshach, and Abednego (Daniel 1:6-7).

God had told the Jewish people they were not allowed to eat certain foods. When the king of Babylon gave Daniel and his three friends some food that was against God's Law, they stood strong together and refused to eat the food and asked for only vegetables and water. Read what happened after they chose to eat only what God approved and write out the results:

At the end of the ten days they looked healthier and better nourished than any of the young men who ate the royal food (Daniel 1:15).

_____

_____

_____

Are you wondering where you will find friends who will stay strong when it comes to doing what the Bible says? Here's a hint—you'll usually find these guy friends at church or in a boys' Sunday school class!

☺ The Choice Is Yours ☺

There is no question that choosing friends and making really good friendships is an important part of your life. Friends are one of the ways God encourages, teaches, trains, and matures you. I have observed that there are three kinds of people in life—

those who pull you down,
those who pull you along, and
those who pull you up.

Be sure you choose friends who pull you up and along toward Jesus.

And don't forget to be the kind of friend who pulls others up and along toward Jesus!

✋ Making *Really* Good Choices ✋

In this chapter we have looked into God's Word and learned how important it is to choose the right kind of F-R-I-E-N-D-S. On this page, write out the point of each letter. (I'll get you started with "F.")

Finding a friend takes time.

R_____

I_____

E_____

N_____

D_____

S_____

Now write out one thing you liked, learned, or want to do about finding good friends.

_____

_____

_____

_____

Take time now to seal your desire to make *really* good choices with the words of this prayer:

Dear Jesus, thank You for being my friend. I know You are always with me and will never leave me. Help me to encourage those around me, and guide me as I look for good friends who love You too. Amen.

Choosing What You Say

Go to your room right now, young man," Justin's mother ordered as she pointed Justin toward the door to his room. Oh, boy! Justin knew he was in trouble the second he opened his mouth and yelled, "Sally, you are *so* stupid! You don't know anything!"

Usually Justin was super careful about putting down his sister only when his mom wasn't around to hear his words. But this time? Busted! Justin really messed up. His mom had walked into the family room just as he was dumping his latest dose of verbal abuse on his little sister. Yep, he was caught in the act!

Fun in God's Word!

Is your mouth ever important! Maybe right now yours is full of metal—which means your calendar is full of visits to your friendly orthodontist. And your mouth is also where you take in all the good food you need to grow up and into a young man after God's own heart.

Here are a few additional facts about your mouth:

What goes into your mouth is your choice.

What you do with your mouth is your choice. And,
What comes out of your mouth—the words you say—is also
your choice.

What should your goal be? As a boy who wants to make *really* good choices, your goal should be to choose to make sure that whatever comes out of your mouth is good—helpful, kind, and truthful.

Yes, what you say is your choice. I know how easy it is to get mad and lose it! It takes absolutely no self-control to spew out harsh words when you want to share exactly what you are thinking and feeling.

But God has help for us. It's time to look again at God's Word and find out what He says about your mouth and what you are to say and not say. Find a pen and get ready to write down your answers as we look at some verses from the Bible. We are going to spell M-O-U-T-H.

Make your words pleasing to God. David, a man after God's own heart, was still a young man only a little older than you when he wrote these words:

May the words of my mouth and this meditation of my heart be pleasing in your sight, O LORD, my Rock and my Redeemer (Psalm 19:14).

What two things is God interested in according to this verse?

The _____

_____

This _____

_____

If you know what kinds of words please God, then you can choose what you will and will not use your mouth to say. Here are three verses that tell you what does *not* please God. As you read them, mark, circle, or underline everything God says you are to get rid of, especially when it comes to having a bad attitude:

Get rid of all bitterness, rage and anger, brawling and slander (Ephesians 4:31).

Nor should there be obscenity, foolish talk or coarse joking, which are out of place (Ephesians 5:4).

You must...rid yourselves of all such things as these: anger, rage, malice, slander, and filthy language from your lips. Do not lie to each other (Colossians 3:8-9).

Even when your emotions are running high, you still have a choice about what you do and don't say. You can choose to say things that hurt others, or that harm the reputations of other people. It's possible you might choose to speak lies instead of the truth. But the right choice is to say words that bless and encourage others—which pleases God.

Look over the three verses above and your markings. Then list two of the things God hates—things that you will work on as you choose what you will and will not say:

1._____

_____

2._____

_____

Out of your heart your mouth speaks. The words below, spoken by Jesus, are right out of the Bible. As a boy who follows God, I'm sure you want to be like Jesus. He always spoke the truth and used His mouth to teach about God and His will to those who gathered around Him. Here's one thing Jesus said about the mouth:

> *A good man brings good things out of the good stored up in his heart, and an evil man brings evil things out of the evil stored up in his heart. For the mouth speaks what the heart is full of* (Luke 6:45).

Have you ever thought about the fact that what goes into your heart comes out of your mouth? The same is true of what you view with your eyes, what you read, even what you hear other people say or sing. If bad things are going into your head, heart, and mind, what will come out of your mouth, according to this verse?

_____

_____

_____

I'm sure you got the right answer: Bad things will come out of your mouth. That is what Jesus is saying. And the opposite is also true: What you view and read and hear that is good gets stored up in your heart. Then, because you have these good things in your heart, what will come out of your mouth?

_____

_____

_____

Are you wondering what you should store up in your heart and think about? Do you want to know what will help your mouth to speak what is good? As you read this list of instructions, circle the good things you are to think about:

Whatever is true, whatever is noble, whatever is right, whatever is pure, whatever is lovely, whatever is admirable—if anything is excellent or praiseworthy—think about such things (Philippians 4:8).

Utter only what God says to say. First, look at what God does *not* want you to say. Just as He is faithful to tell you what kinds of words and speech you *should* use your mouth for, He also tells you what you *should not* say.

Here are a few samples from Jesus' list. As you read along, don't forget to have your favorite pen or pencil ready. Mark up these verses and circle key words. Underline what's important.

> *Anyone who says to a brother or sister, "Raca," is answerable to the court* (Matthew 5:22). (Just a note: The word "Raca" means "empty headed," or "dummy," or "stupid.")

> *Anyone who says, "You fool!" will be in danger of the fire of hell* (also Matthew 5:22).

Name-calling is not acceptable to God. List here two things Jesus never wants to hear you say to anyone:

1._____

_____

2._____

_____

> *Do not let any unwholesome talk come out of your mouths, but only what is helpful for building others up according to their needs, that it may benefit those who listen* (Ephesians 4:29).

What kind of talk does God say should never come out of your mouth?

_____

_____

Instead, what kinds of words should you speak?

Words that _____ others.

Words that _____ others up.

Words that _____ others.

Truth is always the right thing to say. How would you feel if your parents or a good friend lied to you, and did not tell you the truth? That would hurt, wouldn't it? Would you find it hard to trust anything else your parents or friend said to you?

Lying hurts people. It damages family relationships and friendships. When you lie, it means you have something to hide, or something you don't want other people to know about or find out. That's why telling a lie is like building a brick wall between you and the person you lied to. Lies are like walls that push people further apart. They make it harder for you to share yourself openly with others.

Can you see why lying is so harmful? That is why the Bible has such strong commands against lying:

Therefore, putting away lying, "Let each one of you speak truth with his neighbor" (Ephesians 4:25 NKJV).

What does God want you to do about lying?

_____

_____

What does God want you to do instead of lying?

_____

_____

Here is more advice from God: *Do not lie to each other* (Colossians 3:9).

It is obvious, but go ahead and write out God's command to you in Colossians 3:9:

_____

_____

Hurting someone with your words is wrong. Do you remember Justin's choice to play with fire? And do you remember that a dangerous fire broke out and could have burned down some people's homes? Physical fire can be very destructive, and according to the Bible, so can the mouth. God's Word says the hurtful words you speak can be as destructive as fire:

> *The tongue also is a fire, a world of evil among the parts of the body. It corrupts the whole body, sets the whole course of one's life on fire, and is itself set on fire by hell* (James 3:6).

Fill in the blanks to see how serious the effects of your tongue and words can be:

The tongue is like a _____.

It's a world of _____.

It _____ the whole person.

It sets the whole person's life on _____.

Here's another helpful truth: *Do not let any unwholesome talk come out of your mouths, but only what is helpful for building others up* (Ephesians 4:29).

What word is used to describe the hurtful and bad words that come out of your mouth?

_____

Just a note: In Ephesians 4:29, the word "unwholesome" is used to describe talk that is foul, rotten, corrupt, icky, gross. A Christian guy should not have a foul mouth.

☺ The Choice Is Yours ☺

I'm sure you already know that once you say something bad to someone, you cannot take it back. You said it. They heard you say it. And even if you say you are sorry, you have hurt another person, and still have to admit that what you said came from *your* very own heart. When you say something bad, it is a sign something is wrong in your heart.

Like all the other choices you make, making *really* good choices starts with your heart. So make sure you put God's Word into your heart. Then what comes out from your mouth will be God's thoughts and God's words.

And here's another important point: One really good choice you can make is the choice to think carefully before you speak. In other words, control your mouth. Make this the prayer of your heart. It will help!

> *Set a guard over my mouth, LORD;*
> *keep watch over the door of my lips*
> (Psalm 141:3).

If you control your mouth and what you say, the Bible says you will be *perfect, able to keep* [your] *whole body in check* (James 3:2). What a great goal to work toward! And, once again, the choice is yours. You can say mean things to people—or not. You can call them names and make them feel badly—or you can speak kind words, words of love and friendship.

The choice is yours. God wants you to speak in ways that are good. Will you take God seriously about this, or not? If you choose to say what He says is right and choose to not say what He says is wrong, you will truly be a boy after God's own heart.

✋ Making *Really* Good Choices ✋

In this chapter we have looked into God's Word and learned about godly speech. We used the acrostic M-O-U-T-H. On this page, write out the point of each letter. (I'll get you started with "M.")

Make your words pleasing to God.

O _____

U _____

T _____

H _____

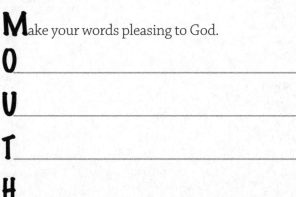

Now write out one thing you liked, learned, or want to do about what comes out of your mouth—and what doesn't!

_____

_____

_____

_____

_____

_____

Take time now to seal your desire to make *really* good choices with the words of this prayer:

Dear Jesus, help me to stop, wait, and remember Your guidelines about my words before I say anything. I need Your help in choosing to speak only what honors You and does good to others. Amen.

Choosing to Be Patient

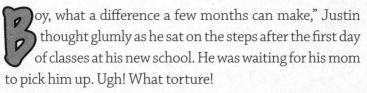

Boy, what a difference a few months can make," Justin thought glumly as he sat on the steps after the first day of classes at his new school. He was waiting for his mom to pick him up. Ugh! What torture!

Over the summer Justin's family had moved away from the small town in which Justin could ride his bike everywhere without any concerns. But now, he was living in the state's largest city. And his first day at school was a real shocker. The school was big—*really* big! He was going to a school with ten times the number of students in his old school.

So...here he was, waiting...and waiting...and *waiting* for a ride home. Even though the campus was only a few blocks from their new home, his parents didn't think it was safe for Justin to walk home by himself. But it looked like Mom was a no show. Had she forgotten? Did she know how to get to the school? Justin waited—five minutes, ten minutes, and still, Mom was nowhere in sight.

Already frustrated with all he had gone through during his first day at his new school, Justin decided that he couldn't wait any longer. He wanted to go home. He didn't want to be stuck here at school! Sure, he understood that he was to wait for his mother. But he was sure something was wrong. And besides, he was anxious to get home so he could play the new video game his parents had given him. So off he went, darting around the corner of the school.

Unfortunately, Justin turned the wrong way and headed in the exact opposite direction of his home.

At that very moment, guess who showed up at the front curb of the school? Mom! She jumped out and ran to the main doors of the school, only to find them locked. Then she panicked and took out her cell phone and called Justin's dad at work.

Dad told Mom to take the most direct route to their home. While she was frantically driving and looking for Justin in one direction, Justin had gone a different direction and was now being confronted by two older boys who were demanding that he give them his money, his iPod, *and* his expensive new running shoes. Justin was scared and began to cry. He didn't want to, but he couldn't help it.

Thankfully, a mailman just happened to drive by at that moment and saw what was happening. He stopped his truck and watched the older boys run away—but not before the bullies had taken Justin's prize possessions. The mailman asked Justin where he lived, and because Justin's home was on his route, he offered to give Justin a ride home.

Meanwhile, Justin's parents had panicked when he was nowhere to be found. Now Dad had left work and was heading home to help search for Justin.

What a difficult first day of school! This was sure to be one that no one in Justin's family would ever forget.

Fun in God's Word!

It's obvious that Justin chose not to wait until his mom arrived at school to take him home. His decision to leave the school without following his parents' instructions had some serious effects. First, he could have experienced bodily harm in addition to the loss of his valuable personal possessions. Second, because he was unfamiliar with the neighborhood, he could have gotten seriously lost. He had interrupted the mailman's day. And he had also upset his parents' workday, and caused emotional distress for all his family members.

Looking back? Justin wishes he had followed his parents' instructions and waited for his mom to pick him up at school.

As we continue to work our way through this book, keep in mind this truth: Choices have results. Good choices have good outcomes, while bad choices (like Justin's bad choice) have bad results.

It's now time to look again at God's Word, the Bible, and find out how God wants you to act when you are asked to wait or need to wait, even when you don't want to. Grab your pen and write down your answers as we look at some verses from the Bible. This time we are going to spell out P-A-T-I-E-N-C-E.

Patience is learning to wait. We might say that patience is learning to do nothing! I know you probably enjoy a little bit of "doing nothing," but this is different. This is doing nothing when it is the right choice to make. Patience is...

Doing nothing when you are told to wait after school.

Doing nothing when kids make fun of you at school.

Doing nothing instead of getting angry.

Doing nothing instead of getting even.

Here's how Jesus explained patience to His disciple Peter:

Then Peter came to Jesus and asked, "Lord, how many times shall I forgive my brother or sister who sins against me? Up to seven times?" (Matthew 18:21).

How many times did Peter think was the maximum number of times he should forgive someone?

_____ times

Jesus said to him, "I do not say to you, up to seven times, but up to seventy times seven" (Matthew 18:22 NASB).

You do the math! According to Jesus, patience does not stop with forgiving someone seven times. No, He said "seventy times seven." How many times is 70 x 7? _____ The point Jesus was making is this: You should *always* be willing to forgive.

Ask for God's patience. Learning to wait is not easy. That is where prayer comes to your rescue. God is willing to give you His patience whenever you ask for it. So ask! Then you can follow through on this command from God:

Be patient, bearing with one another in love (Ephesians 4:2).

List two things you can do to be more patient the next time you don't get what you want or someone upsets you:

_____

_____

_____

While you are thinking about patience, think about Noah. You probably know the story of Noah and the ark. God told Noah to build an ark so he could gather up two of every living creature and survive a flood that would destroy the world and the people in it because they were evil. Here's what the Bible reports:

God waited patiently in the days of Noah while the ark was being built (1 Peter 3:20).

Genesis 6:3 tells us that God gave the wicked people of the world *a hundred and twenty years* to turn away from their sin.

So, how long did God wait patiently?

_____

Take ten. Have you heard the saying, "Count to ten before you say anything"? Or "Count to ten before you do anything"? This little bit of advice trains you to wait—to patiently do nothing until you can say or do the right thing. It keeps you from losing your temper, or hurting someone physically or with your words.

The apostle Paul faced his share of insults and people lying about him. But Paul was patient. What advice does he give about how you should respond to people who say things that hurt you?

> *The Lord's bond-servant must not be quarrelsome...[but] patient when wronged* (2 Timothy 2:24 NASB).

_____

_____

Ignore insults. Don't you just hate it when someone calls you a name or makes fun of you? What is your first reaction? You want to give an insult right back, don't you? He called you a name, so you immediately want to call him a name! Well, patience also applies to the insults you receive.

Proverbs 19:11 says that to be patient is to be wise. So remember what you have been learning: Be wise and count to ten. Then what does Proverbs 19:11 tell you about ignoring insults?

> *A person's wisdom yields* [produces] *patience; it is to one's glory to overlook an offense.*

_____

_____

Endurance is a part of waiting. So how long can you wait? You might say, "Well, that depends. I could wait forever before I get punished for getting mad at my little sister. But I can't wait very long at all when I want to play my video games."

Always remember that waiting is not based on what you *think* is right, but on what *is* right. That's a lesson King Saul in the Old Testament never got. God's prophet Samuel told King Saul:

> *Go down ahead of me to Gilgal. I will surely come down to you to sacrifice burnt offerings and fellowship offerings, but you must wait seven days until I come to you and tell you what you are to do* (1 Samuel 10:8).

What was King Saul told to do, and for how long?

_____

_____

What would Samuel do when he arrived in seven days?

_____

_____

> *He* [Saul] *waited seven days, the time set by Samuel; but Samuel did not come to Gilgal, and Saul's men began to scatter. So he said, "Bring me the burnt offering and the fellowship offerings." And Saul offered up the burnt offering* (1 Samuel 13:8-9).

What happened when the prophet Samuel didn't arrive on the seventh day?

_____

_____

_____

But a little later, Samuel arrived on the scene. Write out how Samuel described Saul's lack of patience.

You have done a foolish thing (1 Samuel 13:13).

_____

_____

_____

Because Saul was in a hurry and did not wait patiently for Samuel, he went ahead and offered up the animal sacrifices himself. Rather than wait on Samuel the priest to offer the sacrifice, he did it himself. In response, Samuel said:

You have not kept the command the LORD your God gave you; if you had, he would have established your kingdom over Israel for all time. But now your kingdom will not endure (1 Samuel 3:13-14).

What was the result or consequence of King Saul's disobedience and his failure to wait as instructed?

_____

_____

_____

_____

Never try to get even. What is the first thing that usually comes into your mind when someone hurts you or when someone does something wrong toward you? You want to do something back at them. You want to get even. But according to 1 Peter 3:9, how does patience respond?

Do not repay evil with evil or insult with insult.

_____

_____

What should you do instead?

On the contrary, repay evil with blessing (1 Peter 3:9).

_____

_____

(Just a note: Here, "blessing" means to speak well of that person.)

Carry Jesus' example in your heart. No one has ever experienced as much abuse as Jesus did. It is very hard not to get angry and upset when someone picks on you and hurts you physically. But Jesus suffered far more hurt than we ever will. How did He respond to His enemies? In what two ways did He show His patience?

> *When they hurled their insults at him, he* [Jesus] *did not retaliate; when he suffered, he made no threats. Instead, he entrusted himself to him* [God] *who judges justly* (1 Peter 2:23).

_____

_____

_____

_____

What did Jesus *not* do?

_____

_____

After the soldiers nailed Jesus to a cross, He prayed,

"Father, forgive them, for they do not know what they are doing" (Luke 23:34).

What was the message or the heart of Jesus' prayer?

_____

_____

_____

Even out your temper. God's patient young man (that's you!) is not a hothead. Do you know what that is? It's a person who does not control his temper. What does the Bible call people who can control their temper?

Sensible [reasonable] _people control their temper_ (Proverbs 19:11 NLT).

According to this same verse, what do people think of a person who does not get mad or angry?

They earn respect by overlooking wrongs (Proverbs 9:11 NLT).

Let me share just one more verse, and it's a good one! Then fill in the blanks below:

He who is slow to anger is better than the mighty [a warrior], _and he who rules his spirit than he who takes_ [conquers] _a city_ (Proverbs 16:32 NKJV).

A person who is even-tempered is better than

_____

_____

A person who can rule his spirit or temper is more valued than a soldier or even an army who can _____ a city.

☺ The Choice Is Yours ☺

Practicing patience is a great opportunity to show your family, friends, and schoolmates that you are a friend of Jesus. When you are able to be patient while others are trying to bully you or are doing things that are hurtful, you know God is working in your life to make you more like Jesus.

There is one Bible verse that explains what you should do every day. It says, *Clothe* [yourself] *with...patience* (Colossians 3:12). In the same way that you would choose to put on a clean T-shirt, you are to choose to put on patience. Everybody is glad when you put on a clean shirt—especially Mom! Well, it is the same way when you "clothe" yourself with patience, when you put on patience. Everyone is better off because of the way you are now acting. Peace is a result of your patience.

Friend, the choice is yours. You get to choose whether you will or will not follow God's advice. You get to choose whether you will or will not put on patience and clothe yourself with it. Try it for a day. *Everyone* will be glad you did! Especially God.

A Boy's Guide to Making Really Good Choices

👐 Making *Really* Good Choices 👐

In this chapter we have looked into God's Word and learned how important it is to have P-A-T-I-E-N-C-E. On this page, write out the point of each letter. (I'll get you started with "P.")

Patience is learning to wait.

A＿＿＿＿＿＿＿＿＿＿＿＿＿＿＿＿

T＿＿＿＿＿＿＿＿＿＿＿＿＿＿＿＿

I＿＿＿＿＿＿＿＿＿＿＿＿＿＿＿＿

E＿＿＿＿＿＿＿＿＿＿＿＿＿＿＿＿

N＿＿＿＿＿＿＿＿＿＿＿＿＿＿＿＿

C＿＿＿＿＿＿＿＿＿＿＿＿＿＿＿＿

E＿＿＿＿＿＿＿＿＿＿＿＿＿＿＿＿

Now write out one thing you liked, learned, or want to do about choosing to wait, or having patience.

_____

_____

_____

_____

_____

_____

Take time now to seal your desire to make *really* good choices with the words of this prayer:

Lord, You know what a hard time I have waiting. And now I know what I have to do: I must learn to wait! I can hardly wait until I get dressed tomorrow to "put on" some patience. I really need it around my house! Thank You for Your help and Your example. Amen.

Choosing a
Happy Heart

Do you know what a crossroad is? It is a point in time or a place where a choice must be made. For instance, I'm sure you have been with your parents in the car while on a vacation. There you all were, just driving along, and then the car stopped because you had come to a place where several roads met. Well, that is a crossroad. Your dad could continue to go straight, or he could turn right or left. There were three choices, and the crossroad forced your dad to make a decision.

Well, Justin is at a crossroad. Oh, he isn't driving a car—thank goodness! After all, he's only 11...and of course, he can't wait until he *can* drive a car. No, his crossroad is whether he is going to choose to be happy today, or mad and grumpy.

It all started the night before, when Justin was on his way to bed. His dad called out to him as he walked down the hall to his room, "Justin, don't forget. Tomorrow I need you and your sister to be prepared to do some work around the house to help me and your mother get ready for our annual Christmas party."

This was *not* good news for Justin. He had big plans for himself on Saturday, and they did not include helping his parents get ready for some party for a bunch of grown-ups.

Justin was not happy, so he shut the door to his room a bit louder than normal.

The next morning, Justin heard a knock on his bedroom door. As he awoke from his sleep and slowly opened his eyes, he heard his mom telling him breakfast was ready. And he was to hurry up. Why? Because there was lots of work to be done to get ready for the party.

Ugh! At that moment Justin wanted to be like that sluggard and turn on his bed like a door turns on its hinges. All he wanted to do was turn his back on his mom and fall asleep again. After all, didn't she know it was Saturday?

Yes, Justin was at a crossroad. He knew he had to make a choice about whether or not he would get out of bed just because his mom had told him to. However, from past wrong choices in this area, Justin knew not to ignore his mom's orders.

But Justin was also at a crossroad with his attitude. He could choose to go one way and have a happy heart—to pitch in with a good attitude and lots of energy, to make a positive contribution and be helpful. Or...he could choose to come out of his room with a bad attitude—to be grumpy, mad at the world, upset with his parents. This choice, of course, would be a hindrance to the family project and take the joy out of their day. Which choice would Justin make?

Fun in God's Word!

Has your mom or dad ever said to you, "Go to your room and don't come out until you have a happy heart!"? You were probably feeling like Justin did after hearing about his dad's Saturday work plan. You were upset. Why? Because things weren't going your way. So maybe you had a fit, and said some things you shouldn't have said. Or maybe you just made ugly faces and noises—like sighing or groaning—and turned into Mr. Grumpy Guy and stayed that way until you were sent to your room.

Wow! I'm sure you know by now this is definitely *not* the way God wants you to act. In fact, the entire Bible is filled, from cover to cover, with God's instruction on how important the attitude of your heart is.

And you can be sure this is definitely *not* the way your parents want you to act either.

No, the right way to go, the right way to act—the *really* good choice to make—is to have a happy heart. So what does it mean to have a happy heart?

It's time to look at the Bible and discover how God wants you to act when you are disappointed, when you aren't getting what you want. How are you going to respond to something you don't want to do or like doing when someone is telling you that you must do it anyway?

Grab a pen and write down your answers as you look at some key verses from the Bible. We are going to spell out J-O-Y.

Jesus shows you how to have joy. There's a difference between happiness and joy, between being happy and being joyful. To begin, happiness is a feeling. Being happy comes as a result of something pleasant happening in your life. When you get to do what you want, then you are happy. And like Justin, when you don't get to do what you want, then you are unhappy.

Jesus is a great example of a person who didn't have a lot of good things happen to Him. Here are two verses that describe some of the difficult things that Jesus experienced. After each verse, write out the problems Jesus faced.

Jesus replied, "Foxes have dens and birds have nests, but the Son of Man [Jesus] has no place to lay his head" (Matthew 8:20).

_____

_____

...for forty days he [Jesus] was tempted by the devil. He ate nothing during those days, and at the end of them he was hungry (Luke 4:2).

_____

_____

_____

You can see from just these few examples how Jesus often went hungry, and He had no home. In addition, He also suffered physical pain and people laughed at Him and mocked Him, making fun of Him.

Now read the next scripture. What should you do when things aren't going your way?

Fixing our eyes on Jesus, the pioneer and perfecter of our faith... (Hebrews 12:2).

_____

_____

Now read the rest of the verse and write the word that is used to describe Jesus' attitude as He faced difficulties and trouble. And don't forget to notice that the word *happy* is not used!

For the joy set before him [Jesus] *endured the cross, scorning its shame* (Hebrews 12:2).

In a few words, describe what you think the difference is between being happy and having joy. (Hint: If you are having trouble answering this question, look below.)

_____

_____

_____

_____

Being happy is what you experience when you are around happy, pleasant things or people that you like. But joy comes from following Jesus' example. The joy of Jesus comes from within the heart and does not require happy things to happen around us.

Jesus shows you a different way to respond to what's happening around you. If you are following Jesus' example, you will want to show joy at all times, even when things aren't the way you want them to be. When your parents want you to have a "happy heart," what they are really asking is that you have a "joyful heart." A joyful heart is a heart that has joy, no matter what is happening around you, even if it is unpleasant.

Take a minute to think about Justin. Your parents probably ask you to do things you don't want to do—like putting the trash can out...and bringing it back in. Or watching over your little sister while she is outside playing. Or taking your turn at clearing the dirty dishes off the table. How do you usually respond?

_____

_____

_____

Think of a new and better way to respond next time.

Next time, I want to _____

_____

_____

Next time you are asked to do something, what will you do or say? Or, put another way, what choices will you make?

_____

_____

Observe others who were joyful. Are you wondering how is being joyful better than being happy? Good question! Well, remember that being happy depends on how good and nice things are. But you can have joy no matter how _bad_ things get around you. Use your pen to write down how the people in the following examples responded to their troubles.

Scene 1: Peter and John were whipped by the Jewish religious leaders because they preached about Jesus. Write out how the apostles responded to their beating and why.

The apostles left the Sanhedrin, rejoicing because they had been counted worthy of suffering disgrace for the Name (Acts 5:41).

_____

_____

_____

Scene 2: The apostle Paul and his friend Silas were thrown into jail for preaching about Jesus. Write out their response to being chained up and the response of their fellow prisoners.

About midnight Paul and Silas were praying and singing hymns to God, and the other prisoners were listening to them (Acts 16:25).

_____

_____

_____

_____

It is always good to notice the positive examples of others who suffered and their response to difficulties or trials. How does the Bible say *you* are to respond to things that are not what you would like them to be?

Consider it pure joy, my brothers and sisters, whenever you face trials of many kinds (James 1:2).

_____

_____

_____

Saturdays are special, aren't they? I mean, usually there is no schoolwork, no alarm clock, no getting up early. This isn't always true, but every boy looks forward to Saturdays when he can kick back and have some fun. You worked hard all week, and you deserve a break, right?

But what if you, like Justin, are asked by your parents to do some work, or go visit your granddad in the hospital, or help Dad rake leaves, or a bunch of other things you think are going to be boring, and you are being made to do them? Think back, and review the examples in this section, and answer this question: How did Jesus, Peter and John, and Paul and Silas respond to unpleasant things?

_____

_____

Your parents and teachers and others in authority will always be asking you to do some things you don't want to do. According to what you have been learning, how should you respond?

_____

_____

_____

_____

Yield to God. To *yield* means to give in or give power over to another. Turn back to chapter 2 of this book and write the title of that chapter here.

_____

In that chapter we talked about choosing to obey. Well, that's what it means to *yield to God*. It means to obey Him, to do things His way. How can you yield to God and obey Him according to this verse?

How can a young person stay on the path of purity? By living according to your word [the Bible] (Psalm 119:9).

_____

_____

_____

In the verse that follows the one above, how badly and strongly should you want to obey what God is teaching you in the Bible, in His Word?

I seek you with all my heart; do not let me stray from your commands (Psalm 119:10).

_____

_____

What does this scripture say will help you to obey God?

I have hidden your word [Bible verses] *in my heart that I might not sin against you* (Psalm 119:11).

_____

_____

A Boy's Guide to Making Really Good Choices

☺ The Choice Is Yours ☺

You have been learning that if you read your Bible and follow the examples of Jesus and other godly people, you will choose to have joy. You will choose to have a happy heart as you pitch in and help the family in whatever they ask or need. It may not be the way you want to spend your time, but it is what God is asking of you as a guy who wants to make a *really* good choice.

Now, let's back up to where we left Justin. He now has to choose how he is going to act when he comes out of his room for breakfast. He has to choose the kind of heart he is going to have as he walks toward the breakfast table. Based on what you have been learning about joy and a happy heart, if you were in Justin's shoes, what would (or should) your attitude be as you go to sit down at the breakfast table?

_____

_____

_____

_____

🖐 Making *Really* Good Choices 🖐

In this chapter we have looked into God's Word and learned how important it is to make J-O-Y a habit. On this page, write out the point of each letter. (I'll get you started with "J.")

Jesus shows you how to have joy.

O_____

Y_____

Now, write out one thing you liked, learned, or want to do about choosing to have a happy heart.

_____

_____

_____

_____

_____

_____

Take time now to seal your desire to make *really* good choices with the words of this prayer:

Lord, I really needed this lesson. I hate to say, I've been Mr. Grumpy Guy for too long. Thank You for showing me how You had so much joy no matter what. I'm going to work on having a happy and joyous heart. Really! Amen.

Choosing to Trust God

10

Justin felt like a failure. It had been a really bad week. No, make that a *lot* of really bad weeks!

As Justin sat glumly on his bed with his head in his hands, he had a hard time remembering the last time he had made a right choice on his own. Usually his parents stepped in and made sure he went to bed on time, got up on time, got to school on time with his backpack, homework papers, and lunch. On and on his loser list went. It wasn't because he wasn't old enough to make some of those decisions on his own. It was because he simply wasn't being careful to make good choices. No wonder his parents had to stand over him all the time, forcing him to do the right thing.

And to make things worse, today is Sunday. Justin realizes he has not only failed to please his parents, but also God. It hits him once again that he didn't do his lesson or live up to his commitment to pray every day last week.

But later, as Justin slid into a seat in his boys' class at church, he realized that he had a much deeper issue to deal with. That is, how could he face *Jesus* with his messed-up life? Jesus must be super disappointed in him. For once, Justin's sorrow was real and heartfelt.

As Justin was wondering about how badly he had messed up, his Sunday school teacher, Mr. Howard, began his talk to the boys from Proverbs 3:5 and 6.

Fun in God's Word!

Justin had always been on the fringe of his Christian friends and their group. It was his choice, of course. Sure, he always went to church. (His parents made sure of that!) And he was in a boys' Sunday school class. But he never tuned in to what was happening there. He lived with one foot in the world and one foot in the Christian scene.

Justin knew he was acting out two roles. At times he would act the way his parents wanted him to act. On the outside he would obey, but inside—in his heart—he was rebelling. More often than not, his rebellion would surface and he would be mean to his sister, give his parents a hard time, and be a problem for his teachers at school. Justin knew he was at another crossroad.

On this memorable Sunday, Justin was having some big struggles. Suddenly he was eager for help and answers. He knew in his heart that in the past he had made a lot of bad choices, especially about the way he was acting, and he was seeing the results of those choices.

Now Justin knew he had to make another decision to stop being influenced by the world and start living wholeheartedly for Jesus. Maybe, just maybe, something Mr. Howard would say might help! So for the first time in a l-o-n-g time, Justin made an effort to listen—to really, *really* listen.

Let's pretend we are sitting next to Justin in his Sunday school class and we get to hear Mr. Howard as he takes the boys through a passage in the Bible about trusting God. Grab a pen and write down your answers as we look at some verses from the Bible. We are going to spell T-R-U-S-T.

Mr. Howard begins the class by saying, "Open your Bibles." (Oh good! For the first time in a long time, Justin had remembered to bring his Bible to the class.) Mr. Howard added, "Turn with me to Proverbs 3, and let's take a look at verses 5 and 6." Justin already knew these verses, but somehow this special morning they hit him hard, as he and the other guys followed along in their Bibles:

Trust in the LORD with all your heart and lean not on your own understanding; in all your ways acknowledge him, and he will make your paths straight (NASB).

Trust in the Lord. *Trust in the LORD with all your heart* (verse 5)—Do you ever feel like there's no one you can trust, or no one who understands what you're going through when you have an important decision to make? It's awful feeling so alone! Sometimes your parents don't always relate to your problem. And your friends are little or no help. You feel like there is a heavy weight on your young shoulders. So you half-pray, "If there was just someone I could talk to... someone I could trust with my problems and decisions. Then I would know exactly what to do."

When your list of people comes up empty, you decide there isn't anyone who can help you. So you make your choice alone, with zero input from anybody else. Sometimes your choice is okay. But sometimes (like Justin's many bad choices) it leads to a train wreck.

You can probably guess what I'm going to say next: The truth is, yes, there *is* someone you can trust 100 percent of the time, with 100 percent of the choices you have to make. Now look at the verse above. Who does Proverbs 3:5 say you should trust?

_____

That someone is God, right? According to that same verse, how much are you to trust God?

_____

What does Proverbs 3:5 say you are *not* to do—which is the opposite of trusting God?

_____

_____

_____

_____

God knows 100 percent of the time what is 100 percent best for you. He knows what is right for you, and what you need, and what will be good or harmful for you. In fact, He is the best person you can count on for help with your choices!

You probably already know all of this. But now it is time for you to truly believe it and apply it in your life. In every choice you make, from the small ones to the really big ones, you must completely trust and believe that God can—and will—help you make the right choice. That's where *with all your heart* (verse 5) comes in.

God will help you make really good choices when you completely trust Him to help you and guide you.

Resist doing things on your own. *Lean not on your own understanding* (verse 5). If you were to lean against a wall, what would be supporting you?

_____

God is not asking you to give up your ability to think and reason. But He is asking you to not lean on, or count on, or depend on your own wisdom. Do you know everything? Have you experienced everything there is to experience? Are there some things you don't know? This is why God is saying you shouldn't try to lean on your own wisdom. Because your wisdom is limited, you need to listen to the wisdom of God's Word, your parents, and wise teachers like Mr. Howard.

This was Justin's problem. He wanted what he wanted. And he was listening to everyone but God. He was ignoring God and the truths in the Bible when he made his choices. Justin was definitely leaning on his own understanding!

Take, for example, Justin's decision to go meet Ryan at the secret clubhouse and "experiment" with the fireworks.

Justin listened to Ryan when he told Justin that his parents didn't know anything. So how could they know that playing with fire and fireworks would be a problem? If Justin had obeyed his parents' warning, he wouldn't have been a part of a situation where a fire had raged out of control. Justin's nervousness and doubt should have been a red warning flag! With his concern, he could have reached out for help from God or from his parents.

You and every person on the planet will always be tempted to do something wrong. But here's a verse that gives you even more reason to trust God:

No temptation has overtaken you except what is common to mankind. And God is faithful; he will not let you be tempted beyond what you can bear. But when you are tempted, he will also provide a way out so that you can endure (1 Corinthians 10:13).

Jot down several truths this verse tells you about God:

_____

_____

_____

_____

Justin got into trouble because he failed to take the time to pray and ask God and his parents for help about what to do when he needed to make a decision. Note to self: What will you do the next time you need to make a choice that you are not sure about?

_____

_____

_____

Understand who is in control. *In all your ways acknowledge him* (verse 6 NASB)—How do you acknowledge the presence of a friend? You call out his name. You wave. You flash a smile and yell out a greeting. Maybe you run up to him and give him a big high five.

Acknowledging God is no different. What do these verses say about God's presence in your life?

> *Do not be afraid; do not be discouraged, for the* LORD *your God will be with you wherever you go* (Joshua 1:9).

_____

_____

_____

> *I* [Jesus] *am with you always, to the very end of the age* (Matthew 28:20).

_____

_____

_____

The Lord is always with you. He is always present, even though you cannot see Him. And He promises that He will never leave you or forsake you or turn on you. He does all this for you. Yet there is something you must do: You are to always acknowledge His presence in your life. According to the verses that follow, what is the best way to acknowledge God?

To you, O LORD, I called; to the LORD I cried (Psalm 30:8).

_____

_____

Do not be anxious about anything, but in every situation, by prayer...present your requests [needs] *to God* (Philippians 4:6).

What are you *not* to do?

_____

_____

_____

What are you to do instead?

_____

_____

_____

Through prayer you can talk to God about every decision you must make. He will gladly help you with your choices. Every choice is important to Him...and should be to you too. So pray with a sincere heart, "Lord, what would You have me do? What is the right thing to do?"

Straight paths come with God's help. *And he will make your paths straight* (verse 6). Your part in making *really* good choices is to acknowledge God in everything and seek to do things His way. According to the verse quoted here, what does God promise He will do?

_____

_____

Some translations say, *He shall direct your paths* (NKJV). In other words, God's job is to direct and guide you—to make your path obvious and straight. He will clear out the roadblocks, remove the hurdles, and enable you to move onward to what is best for you and pleases Him. You will be making the right choices...which means you will be enjoying life more and making fewer bad choices. How cool is that?

Time to choose. Justin was listening, and he found his answer! It was as if a light was turned on. And it was so simple! All he had to do was trust God with the details of his life, and *God* would help him make the right choices!

But there was just one little problem—Justin's sin. He had chalked up quite a long list of sins these past few weeks. "Wow, all that in just a few little weeks!"

Justin sighed and wondered, "How can I make a fresh start with God? Is there any way I can just start over? How can I get my life turned around?"

Then Justin wondered, "How could God ever forgive me?"

Well, God came to the rescue once again! And again, He used Mr. Howard, who seemed to be reading Justin's mind as he read from Ephesians 1:7:

In him [Jesus] *we have redemption through his blood, the forgiveness of sins, in accordance with the riches of God's grace.*

What happens to our sin when we put our faith and trust in Jesus?

_____

_____

God is 100 percent holy and sinless. On the other hand, all people are sinful. Therefore, all people are separated from God. The *bad news* is that because of our sin, we deserve punishment and death. But the *good news* is that because of Jesus' death on the cross, we can accept by faith that Jesus died in our place for our sins. We can have forgiveness for our sins! As Ephesians 1:7 says, *In him* [Jesus] *we have redemption through his blood, the forgiveness of sins, in accordance with the riches of God's grace.*

Then Mr. Howard gave a simple prayer for any of the boys who had not received God's forgiveness of their sin. He encouraged them to pray this prayer, and he reminded them that the prayer must come from the heart and be sincere:

Jesus, I know I am a sinner. I want to turn from my sins and follow You. I believe You died for my sins and rose again, and I want to accept You as my personal Savior. Come into my life, Lord Jesus, and help me to obey You from now on. Amen.

Justin prayed along with Mr. Howard because he knew in his heart that he needed to turn his life over to Jesus— to do it for real. As he finished the prayer, Justin knew without a doubt that he truly believed that Jesus was his Savior. He knew his sins had been forgiven now that he had committed his life to Jesus. And Justin knew something else— he really wanted to do what was right, to live God's way, to make *really* good choices.

Whew—what freedom! All Justin could do was thank God over and over in his heart for a fresh start—for a new heart! He felt clean from the past—and the past several weeks! In his heart, he was done with living for himself, and ready and eager to start *really* living for Jesus!

☺ The Choice Is Yours ☺

Ask yourself right now—today—these questions:

Do I need to do what the verse in Proverbs says—to *trust in the* LORD with all my heart? Have I fully trusted God by giving my heart to Jesus? If you say you have, write down some choices you have made that show yourself, your family, and others that you are living for Jesus.

_____

_____

_____

Are there ways I could be growing as a Christian? For instance, am I doing better at reading my Bible? Am I praying more often? Am I making progress at being a good family member—especially to Dad and Mom? How about my brother and sister? Jot down some ideas you have that will help you grow stronger in these areas:

_____

_____

_____

🖐 Making *Really* Good Choices 🖐

In this chapter we have looked into God's Word and learned about T-R-U-S-T. On this page, write out the point of each letter. (I'll get you started with "T.")

T rust in the Lord.

R _____

U _____

S _____

T _____

Now write out one thing you liked, learned, or want to do about trusting God.

_____

_____

_____

_____

_____

Take time now to seal your desire to make *really* good choices with the words of this prayer:

Dear Lord, help me to remember that I can always lean on You. Whenever I have a problem, a concern, or a decision to make, I know I can trust You to guide me in making the right choice. Amen.

Notes

1. Derek Kidner, *The Proverbs* (Downers Grove, IL: InterVarsity Press, 1973), pp. 42-43.

Also by Jim George

A Boy After God's Own Heart

You've got a lot going on—school, activities, friends, and life at home. And you're taking on new challenges and opportunities which bring up important questions: How do you handle peer pressure and choose the right kind of friends? What if you're having a hard time doing your homework or getting along with your brothers and sisters? And what should you do when you mess up—especially with your parents or with God?

The Bible has the answers to those questions and more! With God's help, you can...

- ⊚ learn how to make good decisions and great friends
- ⊚ see the benefits of homework and even chores!
- ⊚ get along better with your parents and other family members
- ⊚ discover more about the Bible so you can grow closer to God

This book will take you on the most amazing journey you can experience—becoming a boy after God's own heart.